Peter Rees

Why Do Raindrops Fall?

and other questions about water and weather

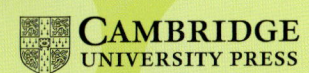

Why is it so? Science

CAMBRIDGE UNIVERSITY PRESS

Why do raindrops fall?

Where does our water come from?

Contents

Questions about water 4

Questions about weather 6

It's a fact 8

Can you believe it? 10

Who found out? 12

It's quiz time! 14

Glossary 16

Questions about water

Q: Where does our water come from?

A: Water goes on a long journey called the water **cycle**. Water in the sea **evaporates**. This makes clouds and then rain falls. The rain collects in rivers that then flow back into the sea. Then the cycle starts all over again.

Q: Why is the sea salty?

A: The salt comes from rocks in the rivers and sea. When sea water evaporates, it leaves the salt behind so the rain falls as fresh water. Fresh water tastes good to drink.

Q: Why do I feel thirsty?

A: When you feel thirsty, your body is telling you to drink more water. Your body loses water when you breathe, sweat and go to the toilet, so you need to drink more to stay healthy. It is very dangerous for your body to have too little water.

Q: Why does a boat float?

A: A boat floats because water pushes it up from below. A boat has lots of empty space in it. The empty space is light air, not heavy water, so the water below doesn't have to push very hard.

Questions about weather

Q: Why do raindrops fall?

A: The clouds make raindrops. They usually start as very small pieces of ice. When they get too heavy to stay in the air, they fall to earth and the ice turns into raindrops.

Q: Why does the wind blow?

A: When warm air rises, cooler air moves in to fill the space. We feel this moving air as wind. Soft **breezes** cool you on sunny days, a stronger wind can fly your kite, but a **gale** will blow your umbrella away!

Cyclones

Cyclones are high-speed winds that form over warm seas. They are shaped like **spirals** with a calm place in the middle called the 'eye'. Cyclones can cause floods when they hit land.

the eye of a cyclone

It's a fact

> We need oxygen

The air we breathe contains **oxygen**. When we play sport, we use up about 20 times more oxygen than when we watch TV.

> Plants breathe too

Plants breathe out water into the air. A large tree breathes out more than 200 litres of water every day – that's enough to fill a bath!

> We need clean water

People need clean water. In some countries the water to drink and wash in is dirty. **Bacteria** in the water can make people ill.

collecting water in South Africa

This is one of the largest hailstones ever seen. Its diameter was nearly 18 centimetres.

> Heavy hailstones
The heaviest-ever hailstones weighed 1 kilogram and killed 92 people in Bangladesh.

> Surface tension
Some animals, like pond skaters, can walk on water. They do not float on the water – they stand on its surface.

> How water falls
Water can fall from clouds in five different ways: as rain, **drizzle**, **hail**, **sleet** or snow. Which have you seen?

> Names of winds
Winds are named after the direction they blow from. For example, a southerly wind blows from the south to the north.

Can you believe it?

Sounds in the water

Sound travels much faster through water than through air. Some whales make sounds that can be heard underwater hundreds of kilometres away. Whales have extremely good ears. They use the sounds to find their way in the deep, dark ocean.

The Dead Sea

The Dead Sea is next to Jordan and Israel. People can float easily in the Dead Sea because the water is very salty. It is called the Dead Sea because not many things can live in water that is so salty.

Up, up and away!

Hot air rises. That is why hot-air balloons can float in the sky. A flame heats the air inside the balloon and the hot air pushes the balloon up. To come down, the pilot lets out some air from the balloon.

Submarines

Submarines are boats that travel under water. They have special tanks that fill with water to make the submarine sink. To make the submarine come up, the tanks are filled with air.

Steam power

When water boils, it makes steam. Steam is very strong. It can move the lids of pans when you are cooking and it can even make steam trains move.

Weather website for kids!

http://www.learnenglishkids.britishcouncil.org/en/category/topics/weather

Who found out?

Why things float: Archimedes

Archimedes (287–212 BCE) was a very clever man who lived in Ancient Greece. He was the first person to find out that things float because the water pushes them up. How well something floats or sinks depends on how much of the object rests in the water and what the object is made from. People believe that Archimedes started thinking about this problem while he was having a bath. He was so excited that he ran down the road shouting, 'Eureka!' which means 'I've found it!'

Steam engine: James Watt

James Watt (1736–1819) was a Scottish inventor. He invented a very strong steam engine. His steam engine was used in trains and factories. There were even steam-powered cars.

a steam engine designed by James Watt

It's quiz time!

1 How quickly can you find these questions in the book? Write the page numbers.

a) Why do I feel thirsty? Page ___

b) Why is the sea salty? Page ___

c) Why does the wind blow? Page ___

d) Where does our water come from? Page ___

2 How quickly can you find these pictures in the book? Write the page numbers.

a) The boy playing football Page ___

b) The hot-air balloons Page ___

c) The girl having a drink Page ___

d) The man reading the newspaper in the sea Page ___

3 Can you find the hidden weather words?

rseltns(rain)lejjgltgalesjentnthailjdnshtnewindkgjenstbreezed ktmnensthraindropsnfjr

4 Choose the correct words.

Water is on a long journey called the water 1. (sea / (cycle) / trip).

Water in the sea 2. (evaporates / pours / freezes). This makes 3. (tea / coffee / clouds).

Then the rain 4. (flies / falls / fills).

The 5. (clouds / sea / rain) collects in rivers that then flow back into the sea.

5 True (T) or false (F)? Correct the false ones.

1. When we play sport, we use about 20 times more oxygen than when we watch TV. __T__

_____

2. Plants breathe out water into the air. ____

_____

3. The salt in the sea comes from the rain. ____

_____

4. Some animals can walk on water. ____

_____

5. Submarines have special tanks that fill with water to make the submarine sink. ____

_____

Glossary

bacteria: tiny organisms

breeze: a light, gentle wind

cycle: a group of events that happen again and again in the same order

drizzle: light rain

evaporate: change from a liquid into a gas

gale: a very strong wind

hail: solid balls of ice that fall from clouds

oxygen: a gas that humans breathe

sleet: a mixture of rain and snow

spiral: circle-like shape that moves around a fixed centre point